Echoes of Emptiness
Testimonies from the Edge of Eternity

Echoes of Emptiness
Testimonies from the Edge of Eternity

Dr. Santosh Kumar Nayak
*Assistant Professor & Head, O.E.S.-I
P.G. Department of Odia
Fakir Mohan Autonomous College,
Balasore, Odisha, India*

BLACK EAGLE BOOKS
Dublin, USA

BLACK EAGLE BOOKS

USA address:
7464 Wisdom Lane
Dublin, OH 43016

India address:
E/312, Trident Galaxy, Kalinga Nagar,
Bhubaneswar-751003, Odisha, India

E-mail: info@blackeaglebooks.org
Website: www.blackeaglebooks.org

First International Edition Published by
BLACK EAGLE BOOKS, 2024

ECHOES OF EMPTINESS
by Dr. Santosh Kumar Nayak

Copyright © Dr. Santosh Kumar Nayak

All rights reserved. No part of this publication may be reproduced, stored in a retrieval system, or transmitted, in any form or by any means, electronic, mechanical, photocopying, recording or otherwise without the prior permission of the publisher.

Cover & Interior Design: Ezy's Publication

ISBN- 978-1-64560-731-1 (Paperback)

Printed in the United States of America

To

All My Readers

&

the Time....

Prefix

Poetry is the seed of silence, a symphony of souls— a speechless song that screams through stillness, a flame that flickers within frost, a mirror that mocks and magnifies, a paradoxical prism where meaning melts and reforms. Its essence is elusive, yet its influence is eternal. In its brevity, it births boundless being; in its delicacy, it delivers destructive truths. At its core, poetry functions as the filter of feeling, the furnace of thought, and the flame of the forgotten. It translates the mute murmurs of the soul into syllables, sculpting silence into structure. Poetry purifies perception, pressing the fragmented self into a form both finite and infinite, both personal and planetary. It records the ineffable and reveals the hidden. It is the heartbeat of humanity, the hymn of hope, and the hollow cry of history. It consoles and confronts, heals and haunts. It dares to distill the divine from the dust of despair. Poetry is also a blade cloaked in beauty—soft in appearance but sharp in action. It subverts systems with a sigh, and seeds revolutions with a stanza. It functions as both refuge and rebellion, a sanctuary for seekers, and a sword against silence. Yet it neither solves nor secures—it suspends. It doesn't deliver the answer but dances around it, showing us that meaning often lies in the margin, not the message.

Poetry and philosophy are paradoxical partners—siblings split by syntax yet bound by the same sacred search. If philosophy is the mind's mirror, poetry is the soul's shadow. Philosophy proceeds through clarity, poetry through contradiction. Philosophy seeks to explain, poetry seeks to evoke. One defines, the other defies. Yet both are born of the same primordial perplexity—man's need to understand his own existence, exile, and essence. Where the philosopher analyzes ambiguity, the poet amplifies it. Where reason ends, rhythm begins. Poetry does not destroy thought—it drenches it in depth. It is the mystic's metaphysics, the seer's syllogism, the wanderer's wisdom. It offers not arguments, but archetypes; not premises, but parables. In poetry, paradox is not a problem—it is purpose. Poetry is the philosopher's playground, where logic is liquefied and meaning multiplies. It is the incantation of insight, the mantra of mystery, and the vessel of vision when vision itself fails.

In society, poetry is the mirror that mocks the masquerade, the molotov that ignites the mundane, the oracle in the open wound. It is both confession and confrontation, celebration and cynicism. Where society systematizes, poetry spills. Where politics polarizes, poetry pluralizes. Where institutions instruct, poetry interrupts. It functions as a force of friction, disturbing the comfort zones of consensus. It gives voice to the voiceless, form to the forgotten, breath to the broken. It distills dissent into diction, and transforms trauma into testimony. Poetry refuses to conform to the codes of commerce or coercion. It resists reduction, defies domestication, and disarms the dominant discourse with mere words. A society saturated with superficial success and synthetic smiles needs poetry as its spiritual scalpel, to excise the illusions and expose the inner rot. It is the scream beneath the slogans, the sob behind the statistics. It speaks for the beggar, the broken, the beaten, the betrayed. Yet poetry is not merely political—it is primordial. It exists not just to critique the world, but to create it anew.

Time is both poetry's canvas and its curse. Time forgets—poetry remembers. Time erases—poetry engraves. Poetry is the monument of the moment, the memory of the ephemeral. It captures the vanishing vapor of experience and cages it in cadence. It is the history that sings, the chronology that weeps, the biography that burns. While time moves in mechanical motion, poetry moves in mythic memory. It is the past retold in presence, the future felt in fragments, the now turned to nectar. Poetry is ever ancient, ever new—a timeless tale told in temporary tongues. It escapes the tyranny of ticking clocks and touches the timeless through symbols, silences, and sighs. Paradoxically, it ages without aging, decays into divinity, and lasts by letting go. It is time's twin and tormentor, its echo and enemy. It slows time to a tremble, and speeds it into starlight.

Poetry is not a pastime—it is a primordial presence. It is not luxury—it is language in its loftiest incarnation. It is not merely emotion recollected in tranquility, but eternity revealed in immediacy. Its functions are many, but its purpose is paradoxical: to illuminate darkness with shadows, to heal wounds with words, to frame the infinite in the finite flicker of a phrase. In its eternal entanglement with philosophy, society, and time, poetry remains the soul's syntax, the civilization's conscience, and time's trembling testament. It does not exist to explain life, but to exalt its mystery, to sing its sorrows, and to scatter sparks into the void—so that even in our most silent suffering, we remember: we are not alone.

Poetry is the seed of silence, a symphony of souls— a voiceless voice that thunders through thought, a still storm that stirs the spirit, a measured madness, a disciplined dream, where chaos finds cadence and sorrow sings in starlight. It is language that listens, a sigh that speaks, a wound wrapped in wonder, a teardrop that teaches, a flame frozen in form. Poetry breathes in boundaries yet leaps beyond limits, its fire forged in the frost of feeling, its heart both helpless and heroic. It is sound made sacred, sense made strange, a mirror of myth and a maze of meaning, where the finite finds the infinite and the particular pulses with the universal. It is flesh turned to fragrance, fact to fable, a feather that fractures stone, a whisper that weathers war.

Poetry is the paradox of presence in absence, the echo of the eternal in the ephemeral, a cage of words that sets the soul free. It is silence screaming, darkness dawning, a burden that blesses, a bruise that blossoms. It dances between reason and reverie, logic and longing, structure and spontaneity. It is a riddle that reveals, a shadow that shines, a hunger that heals, a prayer without priesthood, a temple without walls. Poetry is the tongue of the timeless, the speech of solitude, the lyric of longing, and the map of the mystic mind. It distills galaxies into grains, centuries into syllables, lifetimes into lines. A storm compressed into a sigh, a universe nestled in a word, poetry is not merely made—it is manifested, not just crafted—but called forth, as if the void itself yearned for verse, as if eternity envied the ephemeral. In the end, poetry is the breath before being, the first fire, the final flowering, where the soul speaks in symbols, and the heart howls in harmony with all that is—and all that dares to be named.

Poetry is a whisper woven from the winds of wonder, a flame flickering in the forest of feeling, a mirror of myths, a music of meaning, a language of longing laced in light and lament. It is the breath between beats, the hush that holds the heart's hidden hymns, the pause that proclaims the pulse of perception. Poetry polishes the plain into the profound, turns tears into temples, sorrows into stars, and the mundane into the miraculous. Born in the belly of being, it rises through riddles, rhythms, and revelations—a dance of diction and dream, where silence sings and stillness speaks. Each line is a lantern in the labyrinth of life, each verse a vessel of vision, veined with virtue. Poetry is paradox personified— both storm and stillness, sword and salve, ephemeral yet eternal, fragile yet fierce. It captures chaos in cadence, distills the infinite in a few fire-forged phrases. It is the sanctuary for souls shattered by speech, the solace of seekers, the song of sages. It lives in the liminal, where logic and longing leap into union, where symbols shimmer with secret significances. It is not merely written—it is witnessed, not just read—but remembered. A tapestry of time, truth, and transcendence, a flame passed from prophet to pilgrim, from bard to breath, from silence to self. Poetry is the soul's script, the spirit's scroll, the sacred speech of stars and shadows. In a single syllable, it shelters centuries.

In a stanza, it sings of suns unseen. It is the art of alchemy—turning wounds into wonders, loss into light, and silence into song.

In the serene sanctum of syllables, where thunderous thoughts tremble in stillness, short poetry is born—not in bombast, but in breath. Like a dew-drop dreaming of the sea, or a flame flickering in the vast void, short poetry is the modest miracle, the primal pulse of poetic power, a crystalline convergence of meaning and music, vision and voice.

Short poetry springs from the soul's subtle stirrings—its birth is both ancient and immediate. It begins not in the boast of grandiloquence, but in the whisper of wonder. From the primal prâGa of the Vedic hymns to the fragile fire of a Japanese haiku, from the meditative murmurs of Chinese quatrains to the terse trials of modern micro-verse, this genre germinates across ages and cultures. Born of brevity, it breathes the essence of eternity in moments. It is at once ephemeral and eternal, swift as lightning yet deep as night. Its nature is paradox made poetry, finite in form yet infinite in meaning, muted in manner yet mighty in movement. It does not describe, it distills. It does not narrate, it invokes. It does not wander, it wounds. Each word is a window; each pause, a portal. The short poem sees with the seer's eye and speaks with the sage's silence. Its strength lies in its sacred simplicity. Like an arrow arcing across aeons, it pierces the heart with precision. It does not demand space—it claims significance. Where longer verse ambles in abundance, short poetry sharpens the spirit. In its compact cradle lies concentrated cosmos—a universe within a universe. Its very restraint reveals its reach. In the economy of utterance, it achieves an empire of emotion. It teaches that the soul does not need scrolls to speak—only a single syllable, sealed with sincerity.

What makes short poetry so special? Its symmetry of sound and silence, its ability to bloom in a breath, to resonate in a ripple makes it so special of course. It captures the cadence of consciousness in compressed cadence. It carves beauty from the bare, emotion from the evanescent, profundity from the particle. Its form fosters freedom—*tanka, haiku, senryu, couplet, epigram, aphorism, sijo, or doha*—each offers a distinct doorway to distilled depth. No wasted word, no excess emotion—every line is a lotus opening in the lake of language. It is, above all, a form for the future. In a fragmented, fast, feverish age, where time ticks tautly and minds meander through noise, short poetry offers a stillness that sings. It is the prayer of the present, the hymn of haste that heals. It invites the reader not just to read, but to ruminate; not just to receive, but to realize. In a world of sprawling screens and scattered souls, it returns us to essence. Thus, the short poem is not slight—it is sacrosanct. Not minor, but mythic. It is the flame before the fire, the breath before the storm, the pause before creation. It humbles the heavens with a hush, and heralds the infinite with a hum. In its soft syllables dwell stars and sorrows, gods and ghosts, the marrow of memory and the milk of meaning. Let us then celebrate this succinct scripture of the soul, this delicate dagger of distilled divinity. Let us listen to its light, lean into its lilt, and learn from its luminous limits.

For in the seed of short poetry lies the forest of forever. And in its fleeting footprint, we find the firmament.

In this treacherous theater of technology and tyranny, where the soul's syllables are silenced by scrolling, where screens scream but hearts hush, this book stands as a soft, stubborn song—a poetic pilgrimage through the paradox of presence in an age of absence. Herein lie one hundred and one tanka testaments—brief as breath, deep as death, and luminous as the lucid loneliness that lingers behind laughter. Each poem is a mirror of modernity and a mantra of memory, a spark from the smoldering soul, a feather from the firebird of forgotten feelings. These verses were not merely written—they were wrestled from within, from wounds that weep wisdom, from silences so saturated they speak louder than sirens. They were harvested from hunger—not for food or fame, but for truth that trembles beneath timelines, for meaning marooned in motion, for the divine dissonance between despair and divinity. The tanka form—so brief, but boundless—becomes here an urn of universality, a vessel for voicelessness, a cup of cosmic contradictions. In five folded lines, these tankas hold the tension of opposites: love and loss, self and society, data and divinity, silence and scream, root and rupture, being and becoming. In a world that honors volume over virtue, this collection returns to stillness as sanctuary, to brevity as bridge, to the metaphysical music of the minimal. For what is a tanka but a seed of sorrow and sunlight, a condensed cathedral of consciousness, a language laced with longing?

And yet—these tankas are not only hymns of heartache. They are also scriptures of survival, odes of openness, and songs stitched from stardust. They ask not for applause, but for attention—not from the crowd, but from the quiet corners of the self that still dare to feel. Let the reader who dares enter this anthology not look for answers, but alchemy. For here, the empty becomes echo, the fragment becomes flame, and the forgotten becomes a force. So turn these pages not with haste but with humility. Read with the rhythm of rain, with the patience of pine, with the ache of awakening. Let each tanka be a thimble of thunder, a petal of paradox, a moment of meditative mourning and miraculous meaning. And may you, in the margins of these minimal verses, rediscover the infinite within the invisible, and the eternal within the ephemeral.

In the vast void of modernity, where virtual vistas veil the visceral, the digital dance displaces depth, and the dazzling cityscape conceals the chaos beneath its glittering gloss. Ancient art and ancestral awe are erased in the endless expanse of urban urgency, while the spiritual soul seeks solace in the sterile, sanitized space of screens. The self splinters, a shadow of its true self, as digital devotion drowns in emptiness, and cyber intimacy crumbles into coldness. Beneath the bright billboards, battlegrounds of broken hearts and disconnected lives lie forgotten, while environmental erosion echoes in silent betrayal to the next generation. In this fractured world, a fleeting faith in fleeting fads and a commodified connection leaves little room for the sacred stillness of the soul. Yet, amidst the noise, the true antidote to the digital deluge is found in presence—quiet, patient, and real, reminding us that revolution begins within, in the stillness of an awakened spirit.

This book is certainly a journey through modernity, memory, and metaphysical reckoning. Tanka poetry, with its succinct form and layered meanings, has long been a way to capture fleeting moments of beauty, emotion, and reflection. Yet, in the contemporary landscape, these five-line verses transcend their traditional simplicity to become profound commentaries on the complexities of modern existence. The poems explored here delve into the intricate interweaving of life and modernity, grappling with themes of alienation, environmental decay, and the eroding nature of spirituality in a digital age. At their core, these Tanka serve as metaphysical meditations on the tension between the ancestral and the modern, the physical and the virtual, and the inner and outer realms of existence.

We witness the paradox of progress with beauty and barrenness here just as in his/her life. In the modern world, progress often comes at the expense of the past. The "digital sunset" described in these Tanka poems encapsulates this paradox beautifully, where the allure of modern love and digital connection coexist with an emotional void. Virtual conversations, though seemingly intimate, are paradoxically shallow, leaving the soul starving for genuine human touch. The virtual gaze, rather than nourishing, distances us from the raw, visceral truth of physical presence. In this juxtaposition, the poems highlight the barrenness of the digital landscape that promises connection but delivers fragmentation. The alienation brought on by this paradox is evident in the absence of emotional substance, which has been replaced by algorithmic intimacy—a mechanized echo of what true affection might be.

Another important thing we face every day is environmental decay, the silent betrayal of future generations. The poems have a great concern of it. A stark theme that emerges from these Tanka is the silent betrayal of the environment—a betrayal that poisons the very air of the next generation's existence. The degradation of nature, masked by the industrialized hum of city life, reflects the quiet erosion of the earth's inherent beauty and vitality. Nature's cries are drowned out by the cacophony of modern noise—digital alerts, urban traffic, and the blaring advertisements of consumer culture. Here, the poems mourn a loss not just of land but of memory—the ancestral wisdom once passed down through the ages, now forgotten in the hustle of modern life. This "loss of ancestral practices" is presented as a quiet tragedy, one that echoes in the hearts of those who long for connection to a time when nature and humanity were more intimately intertwined.

Now-a-days, we encounter the digital divide of identity, alienation, and fragmentation. The "fluidity of identity" in the digital era is a theme that threads through the poems with both subtlety and strength. In the digital domain, identities are constantly shifting, as fragmented selves take on mirrored masks to navigate the virtual world. The multiplicity of digital personas is both a form of self-expression and an existential dilemma. These shifting masks speak to a deeper alienation—a spiritual dislocation that arises from the inability to anchor oneself in an authentic, tangible identity. The poems illustrate the fragmentation of the soul as individuals become trapped in the web of online personas, each mask more fragile and distant from the true self. The tension between the self as it exists in the physical world and the self as it is constructed online creates a kind of internal fracture that is at once a crisis of identity and a loss of belonging.

We are facing sever spiritual erosion and the commodification of the sacred. The poems delve deeply into the theme of spiritual erosion in the modern world—a world where transcendence is commodified, and the sacred is sold in bite-sized portions. The commercialization of spirituality, where enlightenment is packaged and marketed like any other product, stands in stark contrast to the profound, silent searching that true spirituality demands. This theme is underscored by the image of "digital addiction disguised as devotion," where religious rituals are transformed into mere performances for the screen, losing their depth in the process. The "sacred light" of true spirituality is eclipsed by the glow of screen-lit faces and the fleeting nature of online connections. In a world where spirituality is simplified into a consumerist transaction, the poems suggest that the soul's quiet yearning for genuine transcendence remains unfulfilled.

Perhaps one of the most poignant themes of the collection is the alienation of human relationships in the age of digital connectivity. The poems vividly illustrate "urban relationships splintered across devices," where the presence of the other is reduced to pixels on a screen. The absence of true physical closeness creates a void—a void that technology cannot fill. Cyber intimacy, with its promise of connection, becomes a shallow substitute for the profound emotional bond that arises from face-to-face interaction. The Tanka poems suggest that in our obsession with digital proximity, we have traded the warmth of human touch for the coldness of the screen. Here, the themes of "emotional void" and "absence" become central motifs—signaling a loss that is both individual and collective.

Linked to this theme of disconnection is the erosion of empathy, which these poems present as a casualty of hyper-consumerism. "Consumer culture thinning the soul" speaks to the way modern life, driven by consumption and excess, gradually strips away our capacity for authentic emotional connection. The "sanitized affection" that substitutes for genuine love is just another commodity—easily purchased, easily discarded. The poems suggest that empathy, once a sacred bond between individuals, is increasingly replaced by a transactional approach to relationships. The rise of digital platforms, which often prioritize clickbait over connection, further erodes the capacity for deep emotional engagement.

The Tanka poems also poignantly explore themes of memory, love, and loss, particularly in the context of generational pain and emotional legacies. These poems echo the struggles of those who are caught between the past and the present, trying to navigate the shadows of lost ancestors and lost connections. "Echoes of ancestors" reverberate through the verses, reminding us of the weight of generational wounds and the ongoing struggle to heal. The poems suggest that while memory can distort or divide, it can also heal—transforming pain into a pathway for growth and reconciliation. Love, too, is presented as a force both tender and tragic. The digital age, while offering many opportunities for connection, also seems to bring with it a sense of disposability—love, like everything else, becomes a commodity.

In the face of all these crises—alienation, spiritual erosion, environmental decay—the poems call for a form of resistance that begins within. "Revolution as inner awakening" is a powerful call for individuals to reclaim their spiritual selves, to resist the external forces that threaten to reduce them to mere cogs in the machine of modernity. This inner awakening is not a fiery rebellion but a quiet, patient resistance that begins in stillness. The final ascent into silence and flame signifies a return to the essence of being—a return to what is authentic, real, and uncorrupted by the noise of the world. The poems suggest that true change, real healing, and a deeper understanding of life come not from external revolutions but from the quiet transformation of the self.

The Tanka poems explored here are not just poetic expressions of modern angst—they are meditations on the fractured state of contemporary life. Through the themes of alienation, environmental destruction, the commodification of spirituality, and the erosion of authentic connection, these poems present a complex and often tragic view of the world. Yet, amid the chaos, they offer a glimpse of hope—a reminder that presence, empathy, and inner awakening are the antidotes to the digital dislocation that threatens to consume us. Through their alliterative beauty and metaphysical depth, these poems invite us to pause, reflect, and ultimately rediscover the soul's quiet yearning for connection, truth, and transcendence. Each poem becomes more reflective, mythic, or metaphysical with the following themes and subthemes like The true name lost in urbanity, Pain as a weapon of creation, Walls, war, and chalked revolutions, Spiritual solitude and ancestral truths, Lunar symbolism, forgotten divinity, healing rituals, Goodbyes, quietude, mutual recognition in strangers, Exhaustion, mortality, cosmic silence, The echo of emptiness—the final truth in the unsaid.

The Poem of the *'Short Song'*: The word **Tanka** is derived from two Sino-Japanese characters: *'tan'* meaning short and *'ka'* or *'uta'* meaning song or poem. Thus, *Tanka* literally means a short poem or short song. The nomenclature distinguishes it from the longer *Chôka,* the long poem, in classical Japanese poetry. While the word *"Tanka"* gained renewed popularity in the late 19th century, it originally emerged as a subcategory of the broader poetic form called *Waka —* which simply means *"Japanese poem."*

Origin and Early Development: From Waka to Tanka: Tanka's poetic pedigree can be traced back over 1,300 years to the Nara Period (710–794 AD) in Japan. The form crystallized during the Man'yôshû - the earliest anthology of Japanese poetry, compiled around 760 AD. This monumental collection includes over 4,500 poems, the vast majority of which are Tanka. However, in those early centuries, the term Tanka was used sparingly; the poems were generically called Waka. In its infancy, the Tanka was primarily used in courtly settings, exchanged as part of love letters, philosophical musings, spiritual reflections, and ceremonial rites. Poets like Kakinomoto no Hitomaro, Ôtomo no Yakamochi, and Yamanoue no Okura were revered figures who shaped the aesthetics of early Tanka. These poets did not merely write verses but crafted echoes of emotion, delicately painted with the brush of seasonal imagery, personal longing, and refined naturalism.

Heian to Edo Period: The Blossoming of Aesthetic Traditions: The Heian period (794–1185) marked the zenith of aristocratic Tanka composition. It became the chief medium of poetic expression at the Imperial Court, and collections such as the Kokin Wakashû (905 AD) and Shin Kokin Wakashû (1205 AD) institutionalized the form. Poetic competitions (uta-awase) and Tanka exchanges (sômon) became symbols of aesthetic sophistication and emotional refinement. Tanka was deeply entwined with mono no aware—a core aesthetic concept in Japanese literature meaning the pathos of things, a wistful awareness of impermanence and the transience of beauty. Through its five lines, the Tanka captured a universe in miniature—a momentary blossom, a drifting leaf, or a fading kiss—all infused with metaphysical depth. By the Edo Period (1603–1868), Tanka had waned slightly in popularity, overshadowed by the emerging haikai no renga and haiku. However, it never disappeared, continuing to flourish in courtly and scholarly circles.

Modern Revival: Shintaishi to Tanka Renaissance: With the Meiji Restoration (1868) and Japan's modernizing turn, Tanka saw a profound transformation. Masaoka Shiki (1867–1902), a revolutionary poet and critic, sought to modernize classical Japanese forms. He revived the term Tanka to distinguish it from the now-outdated Waka, insisting on a reform of content and sensibility. Shiki advocated a style he called "shasei"—sketching from life—urging poets to represent real experience and direct observation rather than stylized convention. Following Shiki, poets like Yosano Akiko, Ishikawa Takuboku, and Saitô Mokichi carried Tanka into the 20th century. Yosano Akiko's Midaregami (Tangled Hair, 1901) scandalized and stunned with its raw eroticism, feminine voice, and emotional autonomy. Ishikawa Takuboku's deeply personal Tanka collections like A Handful of Sand expanded the scope to existential struggle and modern alienation. Thus, the modern Tanka was reborn—still five lines, but filled with new fire.

Form and Structure: The Architecture of Emotion: The Tanka consists of 31 syllables distributed across five lines in a pattern of 5-7-5-7-7. Unlike Haiku, which is strictly bound to syllabic brevity, Tanka's extended form allows narrative movement, emotional layering, and philosophical reflection.

Structural Elements: It has two parts in general.
1. **Kami-no-ku** – The upper phrase: the first three lines (5-7-5), often presenting an image, situation, or scene.
2. **Shimo-no-ku**– The lower phrase: the final two lines (7-7), which provide contrast, commentary, reflection, or resolution. This dual-phased structure mirrors the traditional Japanese aesthetic of jo-ha-kyû (introduction, development, and rapid conclusion). It creates a pivot or "cut" (kireji), even though Tanka lacks a formal kireji like Haiku. The volta—a subtle shift in tone, theme, or

perspective—is a crucial device within the Tanka's brevity.

Let us now ponder into the types and themes of Tanka, the five-lined universe. Tanka is not monolithic. Over centuries, it has diversified in theme and expression. The primary types or thematic categories include: 1. **Koi-no-uta– Poems of Love:** Evokes desire, heartbreak, secrecy, or longing and often exchanged between lovers and generally filled with nature metaphors and allusions. 2. **Zôka– Miscellaneous Themes:** It covers daily life, personal thoughts, political issues, satire. 3. **Sômon-ka– Poems of Correspondence:** Poetic dialogue or epistolary Tanka reflects courtship, spiritual camaraderie, or familial bonds. 4. **Aishô-ka– Elegies or Laments:** This kind of Tanka mourns the dead, time's decay, or spiritual loss. 5. **Shintai Tanka– Modern/Experimental Tanka:** Often breaks form or syllable constraints and reflects urban life, technology, disconnection, existentialism. **6. Gendai Tanka– Contemporary Tanka:** The poems are generally politically conscious, linguistically subversive, or intermedial and their themes include alienation, nuclear trauma, climate change, gender identity.

Characteristics and Literary Devices: Subtle Power in Small Space: Despite its brevity, the Tanka harbors immense emotional and philosophical density. Some key characteristics and techniques include: 1. **Imagery and Natural Symbols:** Seasons, moon, snow, blossoms, insects—stand-ins for emotion and Nature as metaphor for the inner world. 2. **Yûgen– Mystery and Depth:** It embodies indirect suggestion rather than explicit statement and allows multiple interpretations and intuitive resonance. 3. **Makurakotoba– Pillow Words:** Fixed epithets or set poetic phrases used for aesthetic sound and metaphor. e.g., "ashihiki no" before "mountain" (symbol of longing). 4. **Kakekotoba– Pivot Words or Puns:** A word with dual meaning that links two ideas. It is a favorite poetic technique in classical Tanka. 5. **Emotional Honesty** (Urami, Aware, Kanashimi): Personal emotion is central—grief, joy, solitude, and desires are often expressed through seasonal or ephemeral metaphors. 6. **Compression and Suggestion:** The Tanka never tells everything. It leaves space for reader interpretation, emotion, and contemplation

Tanka has its global influence and contemporary appeal now-a-days in connection to human states of minds and various contemporary circumferences. Today, Tanka has crossed oceans. English-language Tanka has become a global genre, cultivated by poets like Lucille Nixon, Jane Reichhold, and Michael McClintock. Translations of classical and modern Japanese Tanka have influenced world literature, particularly Imagist poets like Ezra Pound. Tanka is also used in digital contexts—on Twitter, in SMS poetry, and visual arts collaborations. Its brevity suits the constraints of modern life while offering stillness within speed, depth within brevity, and eternity within a moment.

Tanka has its certain special qualities for which it resonates its enduring impacts. Those qualities are: 1. Elegance in Economy, i.e., Tanka is minimalist yet rich, immediate yet eternal. 2. Emotional Universality which means it articulates human feeling in a distilled, archetypal way. 3. Aesthetic Precision; which denotes that each word of the poem carries aesthetic weight, both semantically and sonically. 4. Philosophical Flexibility: From Zen reflections to urban ennui, it accommodates any era. 5. Cultural Memory: It is both ancient and modern, traditional and experimental.

In conclusion, we can say five lines of this form have infinite echoes. Tanka is more than a poetic form—it is an art of attention, a mirror to the soul, and a prayer of brevity. In a world overflowing with noise, Tanka reminds us of silence, space, and the sacredness of the moment. Each Tanka is a pause in time—resonant with feeling, illuminated by imagery, and etched with the wisdom of centuries. As long as there are fleeting blossoms, burning hearts, and silent snows, the five lines of Tanka will continue to sing the invisible songs of humanity.

For the readers, regarding the poems and their texts, contexts, and pretexts (backgrounds), it can firmly be told that these poems concentrate on human consciousness and consciousness of the age. In the unlit corridors of human consciousness, there exists a resonance that is neither fully sound nor fully silence — a tremor of being that whispers from beyond the tangible. 'Echoes of Emptiness' is not merely a collection of poems; it is a pilgrimage into that hidden chamber where time folds in on itself, where each word is less a statement than a footprint dissolving into sand. These verses are not meant to be read in haste, but to be inhabited, like dimly lit rooms in which your shadow learns its own shape. Here, the ache of absence speaks with the authority of presence, and the quiet becomes louder than any storm. The "testimonies" offered are drawn not from the comfort of certainty but from the trembling edge of the eternal unknown, where meaning is glimpsed only in fragments — in the flicker of a candle before it gutters out, in the breathless pause between heartbeats, in the fragile moment a star's reflection shivers on the skin of still water. The reader is invited not to conquer these poems but to be conquered by them — to wander without destination, to feel without seeking resolution, and to discover, in the infinite space between each line, that emptiness is not a void to be feared, but a vastness to be entered.

Each poem is a doorway, yet none of them promise an exit. In their architecture of silence and image, they invite you to linger in the threshold, where the known and the unknowable lean against each other in uneasy companionship. The language you will encounter here is both mirror and mirage — at once revealing and concealing, always hinting but never holding. Just as an echo never returns as it was sent, so too do these words transform in the act of reception, becoming yours in ways the author could never dictate. You may find that a single line strikes you not as an answer but as a question that has waited in you for years. You may find that a stanza's stillness fills you with motion, or that a closing word opens more than it seals. This is the paradox of 'Echoes of Emptiness': in the absence of explanation, meaning multiplies; in the absence of completion, experience becomes whole.

There is a certain kind of beauty that cannot be manufactured — it is found only in what is fleeting, fragile, and unfinished. These poems dwell in that realm. They speak in the language of vanishing things: the last leaf on a winter branch, the final note of a fading song, the half-forgotten face in a dream that dissolves upon waking. They ask the reader to pay attention to what is slipping away even as it is beheld. In this way, the work becomes not a monument, but a moment — one that will change each time you return to it, just as the sea remakes its shore with every tide. You will not "finish" this book in the traditional sense; rather, it will finish you, leaving you altered in ways that cannot be measured by memory alone.

And so, as you open these pages, I invite you to slow down. Let the clock recede, let the noise fall away. Enter the landscapes within as you would enter a monastery carved into a mountainside — with humility, with curiosity, and with the willingness to be silent long enough to hear the echoes that have always been there, waiting. They do not come to fill you, but to hollow you in the most necessary way, making room for the one truth that can only be learned in stillness: that emptiness, when embraced, is not the absence of life, but the space where life is finally free to arrive.

Electric longing lingers like *fulgur in phiala*—lightning in a jar—synthetic suns sinking behind silicon seas. Screens shimmer with simulated skin, while the pulse of *praesentia vera* petrifies into pixelated phantoms. Here, love lodges not in the clasp of hands, but in hollowed holograms—an *amor absentis*, archived yet airless. The thinning trunks whisper of worlds withering, where roots reach upward for air that no longer arrives. Ash ascends in accusatory spirals, as if indicting the indifferent heavens. The child's question cleaves the conscience, a wound without witness. Smoke speaks the story the leaves can no longer carry—*vox silens*—a fragrant elegy spiraling skyward, addressed not to gods nor graves, but to the ghost of a gesture: a mother folding cloth into memory, stitching silence into every seam.

Beneath neon nights, rain recites rebellions unrecorded. Each drop becomes a dossier; each puddle, a prison of fractured light. Billboards blink, blind to the bruised battles bleeding beneath them. The self sheds silently—leaf by leaf—beneath the brittle boughs of the mirror's mind. Reflections fracture into forests of forgotten faces, none remembering the root. Once, the wind wrote scripture upon stone; now, monks meditate in megabytes, mistaking purchased peace for the *pulsus primordialis*. The Bodhi leaf waits—*patientia perpetua*—for ears unclogged by commerce.

Concrete cathedrals cradle the cult of connectivity; priests of dopamine preach to the swiping faithful. *Salus scrollata*—salvation scrolled away—its password perpetually misplaced. Lovers linger in latency, lips locked in loops of code. The kiss is cached, but the heartbeat hesitates, haunted by the hollow between two actual faces. Meaning once muddied the hands; now it is bleached in binary. The earth's breath is absent, replaced by the sterile chant of circuitry. Mortality pings politely—*memento vivere*—no scythe, no shadow, only a soft sound in the palm.

We grieve in GIFs, our mourning mediated by modems. Isolation itself has been commodified, crafted for consumption. Life begins beneath lit sterility, lulled by the artificial aura of corporate cradles. The breast hums with hope, but rocks to rhythms written by shareholders. *Homo semi-sapiens*, half-human, half-headline, hymns hijacked by history's algorithms, drifts toward a future no one asked for. Yet somewhere, *deus absconditus*—the hidden god—gasps in the shadows of forgotten thought. Love limps through concrete cracks, seeking no sky, only the memory of it. Every message is a *mayday*, half-heard, half-held, wholly hungry.

We wear wires as veins, glass as gaze. We are relics wrapped in unrealized futures, our blood replaced by buffered bandwidth. A life flickers twice in the feed, then fades—*sic transit gloria vitae*. Yet the heart lights a candle, unlinked from the algorithm, burning for the unbeheld. Through the static of simulations, a sparrow sings—*cantus sacer*—a syllable of something unsold. Skin remembers storms; shadows remember soil. Though the suit suffocates, the spirit sleeps barefoot in the fire of forgotten origins. Prayer, once pure plea, now scrolls past unseen. The market closes, but the child's dream remains open—wings wide over waters the world has long since refused to remember.

Our prophets are coded; their visions versioned. They predict rain without reverence, revolution without remorse—forecasting futures they will never feel. Pilgrims pace within profile pictures, seeking shrines built of bandwidth. Silence hides within noise, curled like a secret seed. Ink once carried the tremor of the hand; now words arrive breathless, severed from the pulse that birthed them. Towers rise like accusations, scraping skies that never asked to be touched—*in excelsis ego*. Daylight departs not in hours, but in hue; even the sun seems reluctant to witness our works.

Heaven asks for no credentials, yet we guard gates that open to no worlds.

Our dead remain online, their ghosts glowing in the scroll. The water runs but never arrives—diverted, divided, disciplined—*aqua captivata*. Light pollution blushes the heavens into anonymity. Constellations dissolve; myth has no map to follow. Love keeps time with machinery—each tick a traded moment, each tock an invoice for intimacy. We archive endlessly, yet remember nothing. Birth begins in sterility; breath meets filtered air. Sleep becomes its own simulacrum—forests on loop, oceans digitized. Faith breathes shallow. Idols smile on command. Hope corrodes in the corners of forgotten cities. Each purchase promises beauty's burial.

Yet—beyond banners and broken headlines—a child plants a seed unseen. *Sine testibus*. No likes, no lenses—only the slow applause of the soil. Rain rinses rich and poor alike, yet only the unwealthy tilt their heads to taste it—*gratia aqua*. They gave us fire for warmth; we built weapons. The gods turn away, not in wrath, but in weeping. Empathy burns brightest for storms we will never personally weather. The shelves of life groan with acquisitions, yet the breath is on layaway. Revolutions do not always roar—sometimes they bloom inward until a truth detonates in the dark. The stars once stitched the sky with secrets; now their thread is counterfeit, and our dreams fade to monochrome.

Still, in the marrow, memory moves—an ancient river refusing the dam. Love, when unfiltered, is a flood: staining the hands, drowning caution. The ballot burns, but I cast it anyway—*in fide et spe*—for the child unbroken by betrayal. I walk a city of mirrors, none reflecting the ancient face I knew. Even silence is scripted. Bombs argue over borders, but a mother braids defiance into her daughter's hair, each plait a manifesto. Dawn hesitates, like a guest unsure of welcome. We walk in bodies we did not build, yet treat them as disposable. Time admits it is tired. Photographs become currency, nostalgia counterfeit. And yet—a weed splits the concrete, offering green to a world that has forgotten how to kneel.

The truth smudges, resisting remembrance. The map loses its edges; we lose our stories. Desire survives its vessel. We send messages in bottles to oceans we cannot promise will remain. A single contrail scars the sky; the sea listens in silence. Fear stands between the cliffs, patient as stone. Flowers bloom beneath glass, never knowing rain. Waves return what the last one stole, never the same. Rest can be dangerous when dreams keep grudges. Every inhale is a loan—*debitum vitae*. Wood remembers the forest, whispering wind and birdsong. It waits centuries for the river to carve it into something worth skipping. At last, the sound returns—fainter, older, and no longer ours.

In the cathedral of cosmic quiet, where a hush hangs heavy as history and breath itself bows before the vast void, silence ceases to be absence and swells instead into a gravid pause — a breath before the birth-cry of creation. Here, fragile fortresses flash with fugitive light, their mirrored faces reflecting our restless reaching even as they reveal the risk of their own shattering. Freedom, that feathered phantom, feels weightless until one dares to lift it, discovering that every ascent bears the ballast of choice and consequence. Showers sing to no soul, spilling silver sorrow into an earth too indifferent to drink, while a lone flame flickers against the tidal weight of night, spelling defiance in a language of shadow and smoke. Dreams are traded like tarnished trinkets beneath silvered skies, where desire gleams like a ghost — glimpsed, never grasped.

Stone, silent yet stirring, stores unseen stories, holding history in chiseled cheeks and carved courage, while fragile fleets, afloat on nothing but faith, dare the depths though destined to dissolve. Doorways stand that cannot be entered, opportunities shimmer that no hand will seize. Darkness becomes the guide rather than the guard, shaping our steps with its absence, and time itself tears open — each tick a tiny cry, each tock a drop of leaking lifeblood. A whisper of wind, a fleck of cloud, a timid petition to the infinite drifts upward; promises echo hollow through gaping mouths offering nothing to quench; the dust of dreams burnt before birth settles soft upon the skin of the present.

A span of longing stretches like an unfinished bridge between what we were and what we might be, suspended in air that will not resolve. Flickers of faith blink within a field of uncertainty, showing enough to step forward but never enough to see the end. Pebbles preach patience, boulders bear centuries without complaint; generosity scatters like seed, trusting winds to find the soil of need. Glass glistens with grief, rain mingling with inner ache; a coast bereft of waves sighs for saltwater's return. Binary prophets coldly calculate tomorrow's pulse without wonder, while devotion digitized streams through fiber veins, never feeling soil beneath its feet. Crowds murmur mutiny against meaning; words wander the void, stripped of warmth; steel towers shout skyward, stacking their arrogance syllable by syllable.

Light leaks not in hours but in hues, as though the sun were ashamed to shine; keys are crafted for doors that do not exist; ghosts glow in glass, preserved in pixels that never perish; waters wander endlessly, withheld from their oceanic home. Skies are smudged with city light, constellations cloaked in counterfeit brightness; love ticks like a ledger, measuring moments instead of living them; shelves sag beneath unread stories. Birth is boxed in sterile symmetry, its first breath frost-bitten; serenity is simulated into infinite loops; faith fumbles upward against a ceiling of smoke; worship wraps itself in wires and plastic, calling forth idols on command.

Poverty is pixelated, pleas pressed into hashtags; hope hides under oxidized sorrow while beauty battles decay in forgotten corners; romance is abandoned in plastic permanence; aspirations are sipped on the run, discarded before cooling; effort escalates into emptiness, ascent without arrival. Reflections rewrite reality, showing the face but hiding the truth; solutions search for problems; flames flicker final farewells in tongues only darkness understands; connections burn themselves into ash; music is muted before it breathes; darkness detaches and drifts anchorless. Pain pricks only to protect the bloom it guards; charts chase false horizons into wilderness; announcements are muted into irrelevance; vessels cannot contain what they are made to carry; paths are paved with stones of past mistakes; touch is withheld until need withers.

Eyes unsee what is inconvenient; trees turn from their roots, losing memory in the rot; monuments stand mute, their histories heavy but unspoken; clouds clutch their burden from the pleading earth; heat hardens into petrified passion; frames watch but never intervene; words wander away before arriving; the day's edge holds its breath before leaping into light; bodies are borrowed, fragile vessels for fleeting spirits; decay hums its slow hymn over sleeping steel; time tires of its own tally; nostalgia is sold in snapshots; light lures wanderers into wary hope; truth tattoos itself into the soul's circulation; beauty bursts through blacktop, stubborn as grace.

Books bear their burden long after beauty fades; faces flash silent allegiances to hidden histories; clouds rehearse their pity before the rain; empty spaces are displayed like relics; words are swallowed to avoid the storm they might stir; walls wear weakness disguised as strength; people drift from their places like unmoored vessels; sand scripts and erases each step in the same breath; desire devours without digesting; messages are sent to a tomorrow that may never come; black wings bind centuries of watchfulness; air is bruised by machinery's march; a span of stone waits with patient courage; waters withhold their lullaby; silent spirits survey denied lives; light hides behind clouds yet watches still; flames make final gestures before retreat; growth is guarded from the grit that grants it strength; beaches bring back fragments the sea once claimed; truth refuses sealing, shifting always; faith freezes mid-foundation, sacred in stillness; promises of depth ring hollow.

A small sound preaches persistent hope; dreams sharpen danger; private tides surge unseen; beauty blooms in its own extinction; wounds are witnessed without touch; distance is preserved for peace; every inhale is an invisible IOU to the unknown; soft imprisonment masquerades as sanctuary; wood whispers its wild origins; rock rests in the river's slow sculpting; sound returns reduced, memory faded into something unrecognizable. And through it all — the murmurs, the mutinies, the mutability — the echo remains: an emptiness not of absence, but of infinite, inexhaustible invitation.

In the sanctum sanctorum of the soul's shadowed silence, where breath itself bends beneath the brooding benediction of the abyss, there abides no barren void but a pregnant pause, swollen with the unuttered syllable of genesis. Therein flare and falter the fugitive fortresses of luminescent longing, momentary monarchs over the mutable mists, each ember a testimony to the transient tenacity of being. Freedom, that gossamer phantom so oft imagined as balm, is beheld in truth as a burden, weighted with the gravamen of choice and the inexorable exactions of consequence. The firmament weeps in argent avalanches, though none stand to sanctify its sorrow. A solitary taper, tremulous yet unyielding, inscribes in ascending smoke the ciphered psalms of defiance against the dominion of night. Dreams, dispensed as alms beneath the argent arch of heaven, glisten with guile, beguiling the beholder whilst denying the consummation they seem to portend. Granite stirs with the spectral sermons of antiquity, its furrowed face inscribed with the indelible index of aeons. Faith, like a vessel wrought of vapor, ventures the vast and measureless main, trusting the tempests to yield to the unseen shore. Yet ever there lingers the limen — the threshold unto which foot falleth but never further — a gate glimpsed yet forever ungrasped. Darkness here doth serve not as foe but as fosterer, shaping step and shadow alike by absence as by light.

Time doth drip, not as stream but as sanguine seep, each moment a mortal memento mori, each heartbeat the hammer's toll upon the anvil of impermanence. Breathless petitions rise from the wanderwinds and the cloud's fleeting congregations, their frail orisons ascending toward the Infinite in tremulous hope. Vows are voiced in the vaulted chambers of the void, yet return hollow as shells, their substance spent ere they be heard. Aspirations perish in embryo, their embers commingling with the cold ash of unfulfilled yesterdays. Longing hangs like a censer between the was and the yet-to-be, its incense rising into the interstice of eternity. Faith's faint phosphor glows amid the umbral uncertainty, granting no map yet guiding the marrow. Pebbles preach patience to the pilgrim, whilst boulders bear mute witness to centuries. Charity casts her seed to the wind, content that the soil unseen may yet sanctify the sowing.

The glass pane weeps with grief unspoken, fusing the tears of the heart with the rain of the heavens. Shores stripped of their surge sigh for the baptismal balm of the brine. The prophets of the machine proclaim without awe, parceling eternity into digitized dogma. Faith is filtered through the fiber's sterile strands, unsanctified by touch. Crowds clamor without creed, their tongues restless though their spirits stand mute. Words, despoiled of warmth, drift into the abyss without anchor. Towers speak in the syllables of steel, their rhetoric of reach declaring dominion over the day. Light lingers in hue rather than in hour, as though the sun, shamed, hath relinquished its reign. Keys are crafted for portals never poised to open, guardians to an absence. The phantoms of the screen glimmer in perishable perpetuity, immune to the rot that redeems all flesh.

Waters wander, withheld from their appointed abyss. The firmament is smeared with counterfeit constellations. Love is ledgered like lucre, its measure mistaken for its meaning. Tomes totter upon neglected shelves, revered in name yet unread in truth. Birth is boxed in symmetrical prison; breath is chilled into sterilized frost. Serenity is simulated into unceasing cycle, a pallid parody of peace. Faith fumbles beneath ceilings of smoke, incense rising not to heaven but to wire-born idols. Poverty is pixelated into pleas pressed flat as parchment, their plight preserved yet powerless. Hope huddles in rusted recesses, beauty battling with the slow sabre of decay. Romance rots in embalmed effigies, preserved beyond passion's pulse. Desire is drained before it may deepen. Endeavour escalates into emptiness, ascent without arrival. Reflection refracts into falsehood, the visage shown not the visage known. Solutions stalk the shadows of uncalled-for ills; implements idle without invocation. Flames bid their final benediction in tongues only the abyss may read. Bonds burn to blackened thread. Music is muted before its meaning may mature. Night drifts untethered. Pain guards the blossom as much as it wounds. Charts guide into chaos, their compass turned toward mirage. Trumpets of truth are trammelled into stillness. Vessels betray their vow to contain. Roads are paved with relics of ruin. Touch is withheld till thirst consumes. Eyes avert the appeal of need. Trees turn treacherous, forsaking the root. Monuments mutter in the mute tongue of stone. Clouds clutch their rain in cruel covenant. Heat hardens to stone; ardor ossifies. Frames gaze without grasp. Words wander away from the wound they might heal. The day's edge is a breath before being. Flesh is but the borrowed raiment of spirit. Decay hums her dirges over dormant steel. Time wearies of weighing itself. Nostalgia is sold in counterfeit stills. Light lures yet leaves, while truth stains the soul in sovereign seal. Beauty breaks blacktop with stubborn verdure. Books bear their burden past their beauty's bloom. Faces wave in silence to the shadows of history. Clouds rehearse their rains before release. Empty vaults are venerated. Words are swallowed to spare the storm. Walls wear the guise of might yet crumble beneath touch. Men meander, divorced from domain. Sands script and unscript within the same sigh. Desire devours without digesting. Missives voyage toward morrows unmanifest. Black pinions bind the burden of centuries. The air bruises beneath the march of machines. Patience abideth at the banks, awaiting the pilgrim's plunge. Waters withhold their benediction. The denied dead keep vigil. Light lingers though it hides. Flame strains before surrender. Growth is guarded from its necessary grind. The beach returns relics of plunder. Truth resists sealing, slipping the grasp. Faith freezes mid-foundation. Depth is proffered yet proves hollow. Small sounds are sentinels of unseen hope. Dreams sharpen their peril in shadow. Private tides trouble their keepers. Beauty blooms briefly in extinction's embrace. Wounds are witnessed yet untouched. Distance is maintained for the illusion of peace. Each breath is an invisible bond to the Infinite. Captivity coos in the cadence of comfort. Wood whispers of the wild whence it was wrenched. Stone sleeps beneath the river's patient scour. Sound returns reduced, the echo a ghost estranged from its origin.

Balasore
Dt. 05.09.2024   - **S.K.N.**

CONTENTS

1	Electric Longing	45
2	Thinner Trees, Thicker Smoke	46
3	Incense for the Absent	47
4	Wars Beneath Neon	48
5	Autumn of the Self	49
6	Bodhi Lost in Broadband	50
7	Temples of Touchscreen Gods	51
8	Cached Kisses, Cold Hearts	52
9	Where Meaning Was Mud	53
10	Death in Notification Form	54
11	Manufactured Solitude	55
12	Lullabies in Fluorescence	56
13	Half-Human Hymns	57
14	Love in Broken Signals	58
15	Fossils of the Future	59
16	Deleted Yet Remembered	60
17	Sparrow Against Simulation	61
18	Barefoot Shadows	62
19	Gods on Mute	63
20	Dreams Past Midnight Markets	64
21	Avatars and Ashes	65
22	Graves of Truth	66
23	Blue Screens, Bruised Names	67
24	Petals of Peace	68
25	Where the Soul Still Listens	69
26	The Shape of Silence	70
27	Wisdom Undressed	71
28	Breath Becomes Fire	72
29	Haunted by the Web	73
30	Ration-Card Sun	74
31	Love as Data Loss	75
32	Descent into Memory	76

33	Perfume of Power	77
34	Screens for Lamps	78
35	The Invisible Wound	79
36	Nest of No Tree	80
37	Anthem in Braids	81
38	Shadow's Question	82
39	Soul on a Diet	83
40	Breath Against the Wall	84
41	Seed Beyond the Scroll	85
42	Closed-Eyed Republics	86
43	Drinking the Sky	87
44	The Gods Regret	88
45	Stormlight of Empathy	89
46	Prayerless Presence	90
47	Owned but Breathless	91
48	Verses in Uniform	92
49	Outline of Grief	93
50	Poems for Stray Dreams	94
51	The Wind Replies with Silence	95
52	Quiet Combustion	96
53	Grayscale Skies	97
54	Inheritance of Dust	98
55	Bottled River	99
56	Voting with Ash	100
57	Electric Cave	101
58	Syntax of Silence	102
59	Hope in Braids	103
60	Bags of Heaven	104
61	Ladder of Fog	105
62	Absence in High Definition	106
63	Futures in Chains	107
64	Fog-Footed Fire	108
65	Water in the Bowl	109
66	Forgetting the Stars	110
67	Kiss Like a Revolution	111

68.	Warmth from Within	112
69.	Vanished Godtongue	113
70.	The Hug Cure	114
71.	Tea and the Unsayable	115
72.	Progress Slips in Mud	116
73.	Shadow's Grief	117
74.	Time Offered a Smile	118
75.	Regret's Radiance	119
76.	Name Beyond ID	120
77.	Edge of Becoming	121
78.	Walls That Weep	122
79.	Leaning Toward Light	123
80.	Chalk Revolutions	124
81.	Tears Without Translation	125
82.	Healing in Hush	126
83.	Before History Danced	127
84.	Whispers Within	128
85.	Ashes of Flame	129
86.	Moon of Many Returns	130
87.	The Shape of Silence	131
88.	The Sacred Ant	132
89.	Trail of Lantern Tears	133
90.	Stranger's Star	134
91.	Peace of Forgotten Leaves	135
92.	Flame Between Moments	136
93.	The Patience of Stone	137
94.	One Verse, One World	138
95.	Wordless Awakening	139
96.	We Who Once Ran	140
97.	Tempest in the Chest	141
98.	Oceans Within	142
99.	Blooming Through Blood	143
100.	Eyes Beyond the Mirror	144
101.	The Silence That Holds	145

1.

Electric Longing

Digital sunsets
blur the face of lonely stars—
dreams behind glass screens
seek touch without trembling flesh,
love lost in electric winds.

2.

Thinner Trees, Thicker Smoke

My child asks me why
the trees look thinner today.
I say, "They still breathe,"
but the smoke in the silence
tells a far darker story.

3.
Incense for the Absent

Evening incense burns—

not for gods or ghostly names,

but for memory.

A mother folds faded cloth,

praying to a still silence.

4.

Wars Beneath Neon

Neon rains whisper

on the sleepless city's skull.

Each droplet recalls

a war never televised—

a scream beneath billboard light.

5.

Autumn of the Self

Who am I tonight?

This name, this skin, this silence?

I walk through mirrors,

each one shattering slightly—

self scattered like autumn leaves.

6.

Bodhi Lost in Broadband

Old monk in a car

chats of mindfulness, wealth, peace—

buys silence online

and forgets how wind once spoke

to a stone beneath Bodhi.

7.

Temples of Touchscreen Gods

On asphalt temples

the new priests sell dopamine

and holy updates.

My soul scrolls past salvation,

looking for its lost password.

8.

Cached Kisses, Cold Hearts

The lovers embrace
not in time, but in network—
a kiss, cached in code.
Still, their hearts grow cold and faint,
missing the weight of real breath.

9.

Where Meaning Was Mud

Children chant in code—

rhymes of zeroes and ones, thin

as airless belief.

Where is the mud of meaning?

Where is the blood of the earth?

10.

Death in Notification Form

Death is not the end,

but a click, a notification

you can't undo.

Still, we mourn in meta-worlds,

avatars lit by absence.

11.
Manufactured Solitude

Is this silence mine,

or the algorithm's gift

in the name of peace?

Even solitude's a lie

when echoes are engineered.

12.

Lullabies in Fluorescence

The womb has become

a room with fluorescent lights—

life preprogrammed fast.

Hope still hums in broken breasts,

as lullabies stream in blue.

13.
Half-Human Hymns

Half-human we are,

with hearts hacked by history

and eyes on headlines.

Yet deep in some orphan thought,

a forgotten god still weeps.

14.

Love in Broken Signals

Love in fragments grows

like weeds between concrete slabs.

No field, no wild sun—

just cracked hands holding cracked phones

asking, "Are you still there?"

15.

Fossils of the Future

Wires for arteries,

glass where veins once sang of blood—

we are not cyborgs,

but fossils wrapped in futures

we didn't wish to awaken.

16.

Deleted Yet Remembered

Each death on the news

flashes, fades, is "re-shared" twice—

then forgotten.

I light a candle tonight

for one soul the world deleted.

17.

Sparrow Against Simulation

Lost in labyrinths

of Wi-Fi, wires, and wanting,

I hear a sparrow—

first real voice of the morning,

shattering my simulations.

18.

Barefoot Shadows

My skin remembers
ancient rains, forgotten suns—
though I now wear suits,
my shadow still sleeps barefoot,
howling for ancestral fire.

19.

Gods on Mute

Even gods grow tired

of our endless notifications—

they no longer hear

the honest ache of silence

we once called simple prayer.

20.

Dreams Past Midnight Markets

No time for moonlight—

the markets close at midnight.

Still, my child dreams

of silver wings and oceans

no one dares remember now.

21.
Avatars and Ashes

I change avatars

to match moods, masks, and meaning.

Yet each night I ask—

does my soul still wear a face

that remembers being real?

22.

Graves of Truth

Dead scrolls in temples,

oracles in burned servers—

truth has many graves.

Yet in the mouth of a fool,

sometimes the stars are reborn.

23.

Blue Screens, Bruised Names

Eyes stare through blue screens—

millions in a crowded void.

Yet each face asks:

Will someone please hold my name

like a breath that still believes?

24.

Petals of Peace

Banners, flags, and fire—

so many gods to divide.

But in a child's laugh,

all nations fall like petals

from the flower of sorrow.

25.

Where the Soul Still Listens

What can heal a world

where pixels replace presence?

Only the quiet—

the hush between heartbeats where

the soul still hears its own name.

26.

The Shape of Silence

I wear many names

like cloaks in crowded cities—

but none fit the soul.

Only silence knows my shape

and whispers it when I sleep.

27.

Wisdom Undressed

Books burn in the street—

not by fire but forgetting.

No one reads the wind.

Even wisdom walks naked

in the marketplace of noise.

28.

Breath Becomes Fire

Morning meditation—

the neighbor's news blares louder.

Still, breath becomes flame.

A single thought turns inward,

and the chaos bows its head.

29.

Haunted by the Web

Everywhere I go,

the walls carry conversations

with ghosts of the web.

I search for trees that don't speak

and a sky that forgets me.

30.

Ration-Card Sun

Soldiers of silence

march in the dreams of the poor—

guns shaped like hunger.

Yet one child sketches a sun

on the back of ration cards.

31.
Love as Data Loss

Love was once a leaf

held gently, briefly, wholly.

Now it is a code

sent across dark empty rooms,

seen, ignored, and then deleted.

32.

Descent into Memory

I am still falling—

not from grace but from the grip

of what I once knew.

Yet in this descent I find

clouds shaped like lost memories.

33.

Perfume of Power

Power wears perfume—

sweet as death, sharp as silence.

Crowds cheer as it smiles,

but the beggar sees beneath

where the fangs kiss every law.

34.

Screens for Lamps

Once we lit a lamp

to bring gods into the room.

Now we plug in screens

to exile the dark again—

but never feel less alone.

35.

The Invisible Wound

The mirror is kind—

it does not show the real wound.

That one lives inside

where the tongue dares not enter

and the gods no longer go.

36.

Nest of No Tree

Even in the void

I heard a bird's broken song.

No tree, no blue sky—

but the voice still built a nest

in the branches of my mind.

37.

Anthem in Braids

My nation's anthem

no longer reaches the ears

of its hungry hands.

Still, a mother hums it soft

while braiding her child's silence.

38.

Shadow's Question

Where is the border

between the I and the you?

In the shared sorrow

of not being understood

by even our own shadow.

39.

Soul on a Diet

The world wants us thin—

not in body, but in soul.

Strip joy, mute the voice,

make us forget the vastness

of who we once dared to be.

40.

Breath Against the Wall

I touch the cold wall—

and feel a warmth behind it.

Was that my own breath?

Or a past life pushing back

to remind me I am flame?

41.

Seed Beyond the Scroll

Beneath the headlines

and behind the polished lies,

a child plants a seed.

No camera captures this—

only the quiet future.

42.

Closed-Eyed Republics

Crowds roar for justice,

but silence knows what they mean:

revenge rebranded.

Still, one man prays with closed eyes

and becomes a true nation.

43.

Drinking the Sky

Rain falls on the rich

and the poor with equal grace.

But only the poor

lift their heads toward the sky,

drinking what they can afford.

44.

The Gods Regret

The gods have withdrawn

not in rage but in sorrow.

They gave us the flame—

and watched us burn the forests

to light our own illusions.

45.

Stormlight of Empathy

What is more human

than weeping for a stranger

we'll never now meet?

Empathy is a candle

lit in someone else's storm.

46.

Prayerless Presence

Every prayer I made

was a lie until I learned

to sit without words.

The divine entered slowly

like a shadow into dusk.

47.

Owned but Breathless

I own everything—

apps, networks, devices, drones.

But not my own breath.

That was sold to my schedule,

traded for monthly upgrades.

48.

Verses in Uniform

In the war for peace
we forgot how to whisper.
Even our poems
march with boots of policy—
verses locked and loaded.

49.

Outline of Grief

He named his sorrow

after saints, streets, and star signs—

still, it had no shape.

Only when he hugged a tree

did he feel its real outline.

50.

Poems for Stray Dreams

Some dreams won't go home—

they loiter in broken rooms,

nibbling at regret.

Still, I feed them with poems,

hoping they'll one day forgive.

51.

The Wind Replies with Silence

My name was spoken

once by a mountain's stillness—

then lost in the smog.

I ask the wind who I am,

and it replies with silence.

52.

Quiet Combustion

The riot begins

not on the street—but inside.

One man, one question.

Truth explodes in the quiet,

more fatal than any gun.

53.

Grayscale Skies

I once loved the stars

for their distance and silence.

But city lights came,

cloned their calm with chemicals—

and now I dream in grayscale.

54.

Inheritance of Dust

Memory is dust—

not lost, only displaced deep

within our own ribs.

When you cried, I remembered

my father's unspoken pain.

55.

Bottled River

Love, once a river,

now comes in bottled phrases—

clean, pre-filtered words.

Yet I crave the muddy flood

of raw, unscripted longing.

56.

Voting with Ash

I vote with my soul,

but the ballot burns to ash.

Still, I cast it—

for the child not yet broken

by our adult hypocrisies.

57.

Electric Cave

City of mirrors—

none reflect my ancient self.

Only shadows speak

of the cave I left behind

in search of electric skies.

58.

Syntax of Silence

Even the silence

now speaks with foreign syntax—

coded algorithms.

I retreat to my breath's edge

to find an untouched language.

59.

Hope in Braids

A mother braids hope

into her daughter's thick hair.

Outside, bombs debate

over which god owns the land

where that laughter dares to bloom.

60.

Bags of Heaven

The politicians

sell heaven in plastic bags.

We eat, we digest—

but our dreams refuse the taste

of sugar-laced betrayal.

61.

Ladder of Fog

I climbed the ladder
to success—step by step, blind.
At the summit: fog.
Then I saw the child I was,
still playing with broken clocks.

62.

Absence in High Definition

The funeral rose

from a flat digital screen.

No scent, no shadow.

Yet her absence crept through wires—

realer than her final words.

63.

Futures in Chains

I watch my own hands

typing futures I don't want.

Is this destiny?

Or the slow, numb erosion

of a dream that once danced wild?

64.

Fog-Footed Fire

What is left of me

after the world has passed through?

A few trembling notes,

a footprint on morning's fog,

a cracked cup still holding fire.

65.

Water in the Bowl

I asked the old monk

what enlightenment feels like.

He said, "Washing rice,

and not wanting to be more

than water in its own bowl."

66.

Forgetting the Stars

The world is ending—

not with flames or thundering—

but with slow forgetting.

The names of trees, birds, and stars

lost beneath branded heavens.

67.

Kiss Like a Revolution

Your kiss was not soft—
it tore through my quiet years
like a revolution.
I still rebuild every day,
but no walls can hold your fire.

68.

Warmth from Within

I wore your absence

like a winter on my skin.

Seasons passed in vain.

Only when I hugged myself

did your warmth begin to weep.

69.

Vanished Godtongue

Taught not to ask why—

only when, how, and to whom.

But the stars I found

whispered forbidden riddles

in the tongue of vanished gods.

70.

The Hug Cure

I searched for a cure

to modern melancholy—

found none in the lab.

Only a grandmother's hug

brought light back into my chest.

71.

Tea and the Unsayable

So much left unsaid

in hallways between old friends—

grief with no language.

We sip tea and stare outward

as if the stars might explain.

72.

Progress Slips in Mud

Progress wears heels now—
clicks down the marble hallways
of corporate glass.
Yet it slips when crossing mud—
where the truth still grows barefoot.

73.

Shadow's Grief

In my silent room,

I found my shadow weeping—

not for what I lost,

but for the man I might be

if fear had not built my spine.

74.

Time Offered a Smile

Crowded trains hum grief—

not for lateness, but for time

that no one redeems.

A child offers me a smile—

and the world pauses to breathe.

75.

Regret's Radiance

I lit one candle

for every year I betrayed

my deeper calling.

The room burned gold with regret—

and hope stepped in, unafraid.

76.

Name Beyond ID

The street knows my name—

not the one on the ID,

but the one I weep

when the night forgets to end

and the stars no longer sing.

77.

Edge of Becoming

I do not resist

the pain—it has shaped my name

into something sharp.

But now I carve with that edge

a temple no war can break.

78.

Walls That Weep

They built higher walls

to protect us from ourselves.

Yet in every brick

a mother's muffled crying

echoes through the iron years.

79.
Leaning Toward Light

Even the blind tree

leans toward a voice unknown—

some warmth in the dark.

If roots can still believe light,

why can't we love our own scars?

80.

Chalk Revolutions

He wrote revolution

on his palms with childlike chalk.

Rain came, washed it off—

but his fists remembered it

even in their silent sleep.

81.

Tears Without Translation

No god speaks my tongue,

yet my tears translate just fine.

Every sacred book

pales before a single sigh

uttered without shame or mask.

82.

Healing in Hush

They called it healing—

but I knew it as silence

deeper than the wound.

One breath, one unspoken name,

and the soul began to mend.

83.

Before History Danced

When I touch the earth,

it hums with ancestral blood.

My toes remember

what my textbooks erased—

the dance before history.

84.

Whispers Within

At the edge of sound,

I found a whisper waiting—

not from outside me,

but born within the quiet

I never thought to listen.

85.

Ashes of Flame

I have known hunger—

not of belly, but of fire.

A flame once denied

will sleep inside the ashes

until called by its true name.

86.

Moon of Many Returns

The moon watches me

not with judgment but with joy—

for it, like my soul,

knows the art of returning

after dying every night.

87.

The Shape of Silence

The prayer was broken,

but the silence held its shape.

That is how I knew

the divine had never left—

we just changed the word for it.

88.

The Sacred Ant

Do not search for truth

in the noise of empty creeds.

It waits in a child

watching ants move leaf by leaf—

knowing work is sacred too.

89.

Trail of Lantern Tears

No map for the self—

only trails where I have wept.

Still, each tear has grown

a lantern on some lost path

leading back into my bones.

90.

Stranger's Star

You don't need to win

the world's praise to be alive.

One quiet gesture—

a hand on a stranger's back—

can restore a fallen star.

91.

Peace of Forgotten Leaves

Not every goodbye

is shaped like grief or regret.

Some are small releases—

like old leaves that finally

find peace in being forgotten.

92.

Flame Between Moments

In my quiet hours

I am most fully present—

not to the outside,

but to the flame that flickers

between now and forever.

93.

The Patience of Stone

I touched a stone once
and heard it say, "Be patient."
It had seen empires
rise, then rot—yet still it sat
singing songs to lichen.

94.

One Verse, One World

Though no crowd applauds

the poet's internal wars,

his words still ripple.

One verse can mend a silence

where a hundred speeches failed.

95.

Wordless Awakening

A stranger's soft eyes

met mine in a busy square—

nothing was exchanged,

yet something ancient awoke

in that shared and wordless gaze.

96.

We Who Once Ran

Even my shadow

has grown tired of the race.

We sit down at dusk,

talking like old companions

who remember when we ran.

97.

Tempest in the Chest

The sky was empty

but my chest held a tempest.

That's where gods now live—

not on mountaintops or books,

but inside collapsed questions.

98.

Oceans Within

Not every journey

requires a distant landscape.

Some paths are within—

where each breath becomes a boat

crossing oceans made of light.

99.

Blooming Through Blood

I do not fear death—

only the unlived moment.

So I touch the rose

even when it draws blood, for

that too is part of blooming.

100.

Eyes Beyond the Mirror

Forgive the mirror—

it shows what it is given.

But within your eyes

there's a light no glass can hold,

only the soul can cradle.

101.

The Silence That Holds

I close with silence—

not absence, but completion.

For the greatest truths

are born not in what is said,

but in the space that holds it.

ADDITIONAL WORKS BY THE SAME AUTHOR:

- Aspects of Criticism (English Literary Criticism)
- Dispersed Meditation (English Literary Criticism)
- The Black Feather (English Edited Poetry Anthology)
- The Weighty Words (English Edited Poetry Anthology)
- Ars Abscondita (English Edited Poetry Anthology)
- The Waste Land: An Introspective Commentary (English Literary Criticism)
- T.S. Eliot's The Waste Land: A Formal Introduction (English Literary Criticism)
- Eekshyaa-Beekshyaa- Sameekshyaa (Odia Literary Criticism)
- Toolee O Tulanaa (Odia Literary Criticism)
- Sameekshyaa Saurabha (Odia Literary Criticism)
- Sameekshyaa Gauraba (Odia Literary Criticism)
- Sameekshyaa Prakaasha (Odia Literary Criticism)
- Sameekshyaaa Sanchayana (Odia Literary Criticism)
- Sameekshyaa Sandarshana (Odia Literary Criticism)
- Chetanaara Chitralipi (Odia Literary Criticism)
- Bhaashaa O Saahitya (Odia Literary Criticism)
- Bhaasotpati Matabaada (Odia Literary Criticism)
- Kaalapurusha (Odia Literary Criticism)
- Tulanaatmaka Saahityara Bhitti O Bhaaratee (Odia Literary Criticism)
- Abhishapta Pruthibee (Odia Poetry)
- Soorjya Uinle Raati (Odia Poetry)
- Saandhya Bhramana (Odia Poetry)
- Brahmaasmi (Odia Poetry)
- Soham (Odia Poetry)
- Tathaapi Assiba Pheri (Odia Poetry)
- Gopapura O Anyanya Kabitaa (Odia Poetry)
- Ghunakeeta (Odia Free Form)
- Drusti O Darshana (Odia Essay Collection)
And few other books.

www.ingramcontent.com/pod-product-compliance
Lightning Source LLC
Chambersburg PA
CBHW060611080526
44585CB00013B/781